Riches of the Earth

Silk

Irene Franck and David Brownstone

GROLIER

An imprint of Scholastic Library Publishing
Danbury, Connecticut

Credits and Acknowledgments

abbreviations: t (top), b (bottom), l (left), r (right), c (center)

Image credits: Art Resource: 3 (Newark Museum; Gift of the Iris Barrel Apfel Collection in Memory of Samuel Barrel); 4, 15, and 16 (Giraudon); 11 (Victoria and Albert Museum); CORBIS: 18 (Stapleton Collection); Getty Images/PhotoDisc: 1b (PhotoLink); Susan Hormuth: 5, 26; Library of Congress: 17; National Aeronautics and Space Administration (NASA): 1t and running heads; Pacific Press Services: 22r (Steve Vider); Photo Researchers, Inc.: 6l, 7l, and 7r (Harry Rogers), 6r (Stephen Dalton), 8 (Paolo Koch), 9 (Noboru Komine), 10 (Bill Bachman), 12 (L. Rebmann/Explorer), 14l and 14r (S. Nagendra), 22l (Tom McHugh), 28 (R. Litchfield/Science Photo Library); Woodfin Camp & Associates: 13 and 24 (Leong Ka Tai), 19 (Jehangir Gazdar), 23 and 25 (M. E. Newman), 27 (Mike Yamashita), 29 (S. Noorani). Authors' Archives: 20. Original image drawn for this book by K & P Publishing Services: 21.

Our thanks to Joe Hollander, Phil Friedman, and Laurie McCurley at Scholastic Library Publishing; to photo researchers Susan Hormuth, Robin Sand, and Robert Melcak; to copy editor Michael Burke; and to the librarians throughout the northeastern library network, in particular to the staff of the Chappaqua Library—director Mark Hasskarl; the expert reference staff, including Martha Alcott, Michele J. Capozzella, Maryanne Eaton, Catherine Paulsen, Jane Peyraud, Paula Peyraud, and Carolyn Reznick; and the circulation staff, headed by Barbara Le Sauvage—for fulfilling our wide-ranging research needs.

Published 2003 by Grolier
Division of Scholastic Library Publishing
Old Sherman Turnpike
Danbury, Connecticut 06816

For information address the publisher:
Scholastic Library Publishing, Grolier Division
Old Sherman Turnpike, Danbury, Connecticut 06816

© 2003 Irene M. Franck and David M. Brownstone

Library of Congress Cataloging-in-Publication Data

Franck, Irene M.
    Silk / Irene Franck and David Brownstone.
      p. cm. -- (Riches of the earth ; v. 11)
    Summary: Provides information about silk and its importance in everyday life.
    Includes bibliographical references and index.
    ISBN 0-7172-5730-4 (set : alk. paper) -- ISBN 0-7172-5723-1 (vol. 11 : alk paper)
      1. Silk--Juvenile literature [1. Silk.] I. Brownstone, David M. II. Title.

  TS1546.F73 2003
  677'.39--dc21
                                                                            2003044088

Printed in the United States of America

Designed by K & P Publishing Services

Contents

Silk is such a fine fabric that it has been used not only for clothing but also for artworks. This watercolor on silk, *Promenade of Qin Shi Huangdi*, was painted in the 17th century, celebrating the emperor who first unified China.

For thousands of years silk has been the most highly prized of all fabrics. In ancient times it was seen as such a treasure that in some periods it was worth far more than its weight in gold. In Roman times it was so expensive and rare that people would sometimes attach small pieces of silk fabric to their clothes, wearing them almost like jewelry.

The silk made famous by China is produced by the variety of silkworm called *Bombyx mori* (see p. 6). For thousands of years it has been

High-quality silk is so thin and fine that you can see right through the woven fabric, like this silk fabric embroidered with decorative figures, flying over a display at a silkmaking festival in 2002.

used to make clothing, artworks, and many other objects.

High-quality silk can create a fabric so light and airy that you can see right through it. (People in early India called it "woven wind.") However, fine silks are also used to create a wide variety of heavier fabrics, such as satins and brocades.

Whether light or heavy, silk has always been sought for its soft, smooth, enduring beauty. For many centuries the most beautiful clothing of all has been made from this fabric. Beyond that, great artists have painted, dyed, and printed patterns on silk, producing some of the finest artworks ever created. Silk fabrics have been used in many other ways, too, including altar hangings, banners, and draperies of all kinds.

Silk has also played a major role in history, as a key item sold on the Silk Road, the great trading route that crossed Asia (see p. 15). Running from China to the Mediterranean, this route linked the greatest civilizations of the ancient world.

Today silk plays a less central role than in ancient times. For many kinds of uses, it has been replaced by nylon and other synthetic (human-made) fabrics.

However, silk is still the ultimate in luxury, the standard against which all other fabrics are measured. It remains a highly prized, very expensive clothing fabric. That is partly because of its glamorous history. The enduring appeal of silk is a combination of its history and the qualities it brings to clothing, furnishings, and artworks.

The silkworm above is just beginning the process of spinning its cocoon in a mulberry tree.
At right it has gone further in the process. The shiny white filament (thin thread of silk) it is spinning will become the highly treasured silk fabric.

What Is Silk?

Chinese legends tell of Lei Zi, wife of Chinese emperor Huang Di. While she was wandering in her garden, a silkworm's cocoon (its temporary protective shelter) fell from a mulberry tree into her cup of tea. Idly fingering the cocoon, she found that it unwound into a thin thread. In the process she discovered silk and came to be called the Lady of the Silkworm.

The tale is a legend, but the details are true to life. The silk made famous by China is a threadlike fiber produced by a caterpillar we know as the *silkworm*.

The silkworm is actually one stage in the life of a moth biologists call *Bombyx mori*. The life cycle starts when the moth lays eggs. These hatch into silkworms (*larvae*), which grow by feeding on the leaves of mulberry trees.

In the second stage of its life the silkworm weaves its cocoon. It does this by producing liquid from two glands (*spinnerets*) below its mouth. When it comes into contact with the

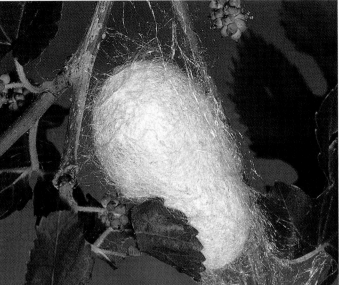

(Left) This is a finished *Bombyx mori* silkworm cocoon, resting among twigs in a mulberry tree. The silkworm inside it is in the process of changing into a moth.

(Right) This *Bombyx mori* moth has just emerged from the top of its white cocoon, on which it is resting.

air, the liquid becomes a solid, forming the threadlike silk fiber.

Moving its head from side to side, the silkworm winds the silk around itself in a figure-eight pattern. At the start the silk thread is transparent—that is, we can see through it. As the layers accumulate, the cocoon becomes white and opaque (not transparent).

The continuous silk thread (*filament*) can be as much as 2,000 to 3,000 feet (about 600 to 900 meters) long. However, it is extremely thin, only about 30 microns (30 thousandths of a millimeter) wide. That is only a third as thick as a sheet of newspaper!

Inside the cocoon the caterpillar develops into a moth. If left untouched, the moth inside will break out of the cocoon (after producing a chemical to dissolve the threads at one end). However, broken silken threads are much less valuable. To keep the silk thread unbroken, people who cultivate (deliberately grow) silkworms kill most of the moths before they burst out of the cocoon.

Beautifully colored silk threads have long been used for embroidering designs on high-quality silk cloth, as this young Chinese woman is doing.

The Silken Thread

The silk thread produced by the silkworm is made of *proteins*. Part of every living cell, proteins are made up of the elements (basic substances) carbon, hydrogen, oxygen, nitrogen, and often sulfur. The main protein in silk is called *fibroin*. The fibroin is coated with another protein called *sericin*. This gumlike substance holds the winding thread together in the cocoon.

Fibroin does not dissolve in water, but sericin does. When the silkworm's cocoon is dipped in hot water, some of the sericin dissolves. This allows the long, thin silk filament to be unwound, as Lei Zi did in the legend. The result is called *raw silk*. The rest of the sericin is removed during later processing (see p. 23).

Silk is the only natural fiber that is created as thread. However, it is too thin for use as is, so several silk filaments are wound together into thicker threads or yarns. These are later used for creating cloth (see p. 27). Other natural fabrics, such as cotton and wool, must be spun into thread. That is also done with broken silk filaments (see p. 24).

Qualities of Silk

Silk is remarkably strong, by far the strongest of all the natural fabrics. However, it is also very light. Those qualities make it possible to produce silk cloth that is strong, yet sheer (so thin and fine that you can see through it). Before the invention of nylon in the mid-1900s, sheer silk stockings were the ultimate in luxury.

Silk is favored in many settings where weight and strength are important. For example, jockeys and cyclists

have long favored silk for their uniforms. (Jockeys' clothes are often called *silks*.) Right through World War II, parachutes were often made of silk. Indeed, silk is so lightweight that, for some purposes, chemicals are added to make it heavier, a process called *weighting*.

Silk has excellent *elasticity* and *resilience* (ability to stretch and then return to its original length). It is also

Homeland of silk, China also has long and old traditions of embroidering silk, often with regional variations. This embroidered silk cloth is from Hangzhou on the eastern Chinese coast.

One of silk's greatest attractions is that it can be dyed many brilliant colors, as in this young Indian girl's dress (*sari*). In early times silk dyed purple was so rare and valuable that only people in royal families were allowed to wear it.

soft and smooth, feeling luxurious on the body. It resists *mildew* (a fungus that attacks some other natural fabrics) and is not likely to be damaged by moths (as wool is). In addition, it handles both heat and cold well. It can absorb a good deal of moisture without feeling damp (though it loses some of its strength when wet). These practical qualities make silk one of the most comfortable and durable of all the clothing fabrics.

Silk is also the most beautiful of all the natural fabrics. It has *luster*— that is, it shines with reflected light— and drapes beautifully. In addition, silk takes colors very well and can be dyed and printed in an enormous range of hues. As a result, silk is a first choice of many of the world's greatest designers.

Silk has always been one of the most expensive fabrics. This is because great labor goes into producing the silken threads (see p. 23). It also requires great care. It can be harmed by sunlight or excessive heat, and high-quality silks are usually best dry-cleaned, rather than washed by hand.

Wild Silks

Some other insects, including certain caterpillars and spiders, also

Silk has long been favored for glamorous evening gowns. This one, dating from 1908, is made of satin (a special silk weave) with panels of different kinds of silk fabric.

produce threadlike fibers. Many such fibers are not suitable for making into cloth, but a few are. These are called *wild silks* (though most are actually not wild but come from cultivated silk moths).

The most common wild silk is *tussah silk.* Unlike the fine, white *Bombyx mori* fibers, tussah silk is normally a yellowish brown. *Muga silk,* primarily produced in India, is also naturally a yellowish color. The color of silk depends on the silk-worms' diet. The tussah moths, for example, eat primarily oak leaves, rather than the mulberry leaves preferred by the *Bombyx mori* silkworm.

Wild silks are rougher than fine silks. This is because the moths generally burst out of their cocoons, breaking the silk fibers into small pieces. Though they are inferior to the finest silks, wild silks are produced in many parts of the world, especially in India.

In modern silk production the silkworms are often raised in large trays or boxes. In this Vietnamese factory the silkworms are being spread out on a tray full of fresh, young mulberry leaves for them to eat.

Making Silk

Silk is created by the silkworm (see p. 6). However, humans have controlled silk production for more than 4,500 years, cultivating the silkworms so they will create the finest silk. This process is called *sericulture* (*serica* was an early Greek word for silk).

The process starts with the *Bombyx mori* moth laying its eggs. Normally this happens just once a year. The eggs are laid on mulberry twigs in the autumn and lie dormant (sleeping) over the winter. Silkworms emerge from the eggs in the spring, when mulberry trees begin to put out young, fresh leaves for them to eat. The silkworms' emergence is triggered by warmer temperatures and more light.

Today many silkworm moths lay their eggs in factories. There silk workers control the temperature and amount of light so the eggs hatch

Workers pick young mulberry leaves from trees in a field. The leaves are then taken to the silkmaking factory and fed to the silkworms on their trays.

only when mulberry leaves are available to feed the silkworms. When enough food is available, workers may adjust temperature and light to produce several generations of silkworms in a year, not just one.

Whether in a private home or a factory, the silkworms are usually placed on large trays or in open boxes and kept in sheltered areas with plenty of air and controlled temperature. Workers pick leaves from mulberry trees and spread them on the trays for the silkworms to eat. Only about one millimeter (about .04 inches) long at the start, each silkworm will grow to 70 or 80 times that size, to about three inches, over the next five weeks.

During this time the silkworms are constantly eating. A factory full of silkworms eating mulberry leaves is said to sound like a very heavy rainstorm. To get one kilogram (2.2 pounds) of silk, workers must supply silkworms with about 220 kilograms (485 pounds) of mulberry leaves!

When the caterpillar has grown to its full size, it seeks a place to build its cocoon. Caterpillars usually prefer to build cocoons on mulberry twigs. However, silk workers often provide other cocoon-building places, anything from a set of tiny boxes to an old broom with spread-apart straws. The actual spinning of the cocoon takes about two to three days (see p. 6).

When the cocoons are complete, silk workers sort them by size and quality. Some cocoons are set aside so the moths inside can lay eggs for the next generation of silkworms. The rest of the cocoons are heated to kill (*stifle*) the moths inside and prevent them from breaking out of the cocoon. The heat also dries out the cocoons. These can then be stored, sometimes for months, until workers are ready to unwind them (see p. 22).

Though many silk-spinning moths exist in the wild, *Bombyx mori* moths no longer do. They are utterly dependent on humans, who have for thousands of years handled every stage of their life and death. The moths can no longer fly, and even the caterpillars are unable to travel very far.

Other silk-producing moths are not so completely dependent on humans and are more usually cultivated near private homes than in factories. However, their life cycle is similar.

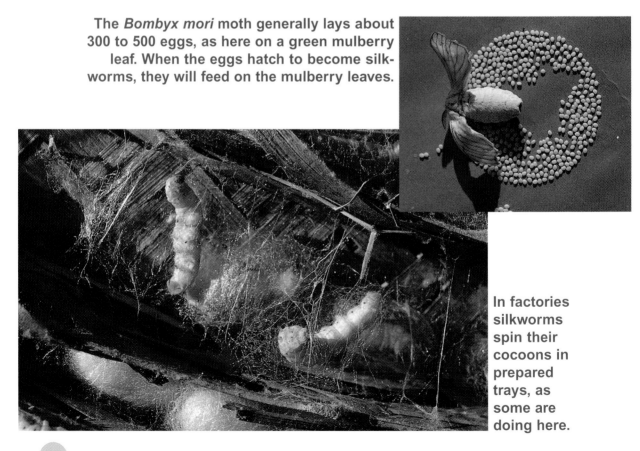

The *Bombyx mori* moth generally lays about 300 to 500 eggs, as here on a green mulberry leaf. When the eggs hatch to become silkworms, they will feed on the mulberry leaves.

In factories silkworms spin their cocoons in prepared trays, as some are doing here.

Silk in History

For many centuries all silk originated in China. In caravans like this one painted by Alexandre Gabriel Decamps, the silk passed from trader to trader across thousands of miles of desert and mountains to reach western Asia, Europe, and northern Africa.

We do not know who discovered silk or exactly when, but we certainly know where. The discovery is traditionally credited to Lei Zi (see p. 6). However, many Chinese discoveries were credited to ruling families, rather than to the true discoverers.

Lei Zi was supposed to have made her discovery in around 2640 B.C. The actual discovery of silk may have been earlier than this, since some fragments of silk have been tentatively dated to as early as 3000 B.C.

We are, however, certain that China is the home of silkmaking.

Not only that, but the Chinese kept the secret of silkmaking to themselves for thousands of years.

From very early times silk was an important part of Chinese life. Part of each property was set aside for growing mulberry trees to feed the silkworms. In every family, from the poorest to the richest, the women were responsible for cultivating the silkworms and creating skeins (loose coils) of silk threads from the filaments (see p. 22). The fortunes of the family depended on this work, for taxes were often paid in silk skeins.

During much of Chinese history,

15

Much of a Chinese family's fortunes traditionally depended on silkmaking, and every piece of property had a certain amount of land set aside for mulberry trees to feed the silkworms. This painting from the early 1800s shows a family sorting silkworm cocoons.

the silk skeins would be sent to government-run workshops, where the silk would be woven into fabric. From very early times bolts (large rolls) of silk fabric were traded westward from China into Central Asia. Going from one trader to another, silk fabric eventually reached all the way across Asia, a distance of some 5,000 miles. The route it followed came to be called the Silk Road.

We do not know exactly when silk first reached the Mediterranean region. The Greeks of Alexander the Great's time in the 300s B.C. certainly knew about silk. In fact, they gave us our name for the fabric. They called it *serica*, which later became *silk*. Silk also traveled west and then south into India, east to Japan, and northwest into eastern Europe. But the heart of Western civilization in early times was the Mediterranean, which was the Western end of the Silk Road.

The silk exported from China in this period was generally undyed and so sheer that you could see right through it. In the first century A.D. the Roman writer Pliny complained that silk was brought from "the ends of the earth" so a Roman woman "may exhibit her charms in transparent gauze." A later visitor to China noted that he could see a mole on the chest of an officer through five layers of silk!

On the shores of the Mediterranean color was added to the silk. The Phoenicians in what is now Lebanon made special purple dyes—actually ranging from deep red to inky black—from certain shellfish. The resulting purple silks were so rare and expensive that only royalty could wear them. That is the origin of the phrases "royal purple" or "born to the purple."

During these centuries silk was the main export of China. Even in the great days of the Roman Empire, other countries had little of interest to China. Much gold was drained from the West to pay for China's fabulous silks.

In some periods silk was so valuable that it was worth more than its weight in gold. People in other countries would sometimes unravel imported silks and reweave the

Following a tradition going back thousands of years, this merchant from the early 1900s is selling fabrics of silk, wool, and cotton in Samarkand, once a great city on the Silk Road, now part of independent Uzbekistan.

After many centuries Europeans learned the secrets of silkmaking. Then they could make both the heavy satin blanket covering this baby's body and the sheer silk fabric covering its face in Hubert Salentin's painting *The Return from the Christening*.

threads with cotton, wool, or linen, to create more fabrics containing silk.

Still the Chinese kept their secrets for centuries. Not until about 550 A.D. did Westerners learn that silk came from the mulberry-fed silkworm. That was when two Persian monks reportedly smuggled silkworms out of China in hollow bamboo canes. However, Westerners did not know some of the key secrets of silkmaking, such as how to keep the moth from breaking open the cocoon, until later, perhaps not until the mid-700s.

Gradually cultivation of silk spread into Europe, centered first in Italy and, from the late 1400s, in France. Over the centuries Europeans came to make silks as fine as those from China, including the high-quality silk gowns worn by the rich and royal. However, the countries of Asia would continue to dominate silk production.

In modern times India has become a major producer of silk fabrics, like the beautiful materials on display here. Some of these are made of "wild" silks, rather than the high-quality silk from the *Bombyx mori* silkworm.

Silk around the World

For thousands of years China was the only silk-producing country in the world. Silk traveled thousands of miles across Asia, through mountains, deserts, and other bandit-held regions, to reach markets in western Asia, Europe, and Africa. No matter how dangerous the route and how costly the fabric, demand for silk remained high. Meanwhile the se-crets of silkmaking continued to be held by China until about 1,500 years ago (see p. 18).

Yet those secrets are not very complicated. Then as now, silk farming requires only a moderate climate, good soil for growing mulberry trees, and a large workforce willing to work for little pay. In the end the Chinese-held secrets of silk

19

After the secret of silkmaking reached western Asia and Europe, silk was more widely used for many purposes. These are banners in the Shrine of the Holy Sepulchre in Jerusalem, as painted in the 1800s by David Roberts.

production spread to others. Then many countries began making silk, some in large quantities.

In eastern Asia, Japan and Korea developed their own large silk industries. In southern Asia, India became a major silk producer, mainly of such wild silks as the muga and tussah varieties (see p. 10). Several countries in southeastern Asia also became silk producers. In central and western Asia, Persia (now Iran) also became a major silk producer, as did other countries along the several routes of the Silk Road.

Today silk is grown in many countries throughout the world, but China is still by far the world's greatest silk producer. In the 1990s its 30,000 tons of silk per year amounted to half of the world's silk production. Most Chinese silk is of the fine white variety from the *Bombyx mori* (see p. 6), though

smaller quantities of other silks are also produced.

Japan and India are also substantial silk producers. Most Japanese silk is also of the fine white *Bombyx mori* variety. Silks produced in India today are still called wild silks. However, the silkworms are no longer really wild but have long been cultivated in thousands of India's villages. Almost all of India's raw silk is used to make clothing

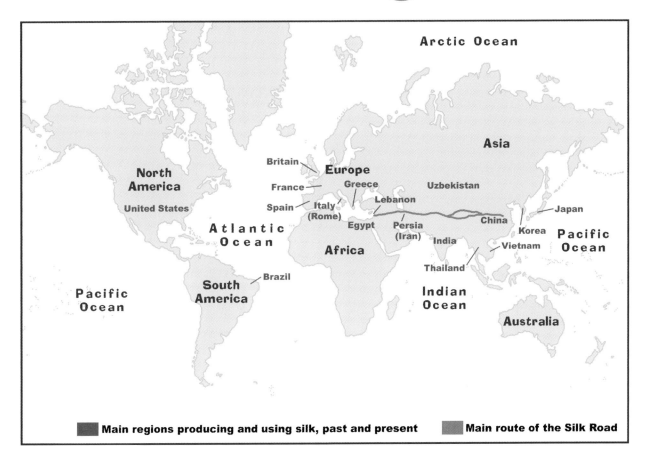

Arctic Ocean

Asia

Britain

Europe

France

Greece

Uzbekistan

North
America

United States

Spain

Italy
(Rome)

Lebanon

Japan

Egypt

Persia
(Iran)

China

Korea

Atlantic
Ocean

India

Pacific
Ocean

Africa

Vietnam

Pacific
Ocean

Brazil

South
America

Thailand

Indian
Ocean

Australia

Main regions producing and using silk, past and present   Main route of the Silk Road

and other silk products in India. These are then either sold in India or exported for sale abroad. Silken Indian *saris* (dresses) are especially prized. Other Asian countries that produce large amounts of silk include Thailand, South Korea, and Uzbekistan.

European silk production has dropped off in modern times. That is partly because Asian silks have become less expensive than those produced in Europe. Silk has also been widely replaced by synthetic fabrics. Yet substantial amounts of silk are still produced in Italy and France, and smaller amounts in several other European countries.

In the Americas Brazil is a large-scale silk producer. The United States produces little silk of its own. However, it is one of the world's leading silk manufacturers, using much imported silk in its fashion, clothing, and home furnishings industries.

This cocoon is spun from a silk filament that can be used to make the much-prized silk fabric.

Silk is woven into many kinds of fabrics for different uses, as in this gold-colored silk kimono and accompanying silk-covered hand-bag, all of beautiful, lustrous colors.

From Cocoon to Cloth

The silk-manufacturing process begins when the silkworm cocoons arrive at a silk factory (called a *filature*). At the factory the first step is to sort the cocoons by color and quality.

The desired cocoons are made of long, thin, unbroken filaments of silk (see p. 6). Cocoons that cannot be unwound into long, continuous filaments are set aside during the sorting process. These include cocoons that were damaged or are misshapen, those with holes made by escaping silk moths, and double cocoons. Such cocoons are later used for spinning silk yarn (see p. 24).

What remains after sorting are cocoons that can be unwound into long, continuous filaments. These cocoons then enter the process called *reeling*.

Reeling

The aim in reeling is to unwind the tightly packed silk of the cocoons without breaking the silk filaments. To do that best, the cocoons are first softened by soaking them in several hot and cold soapy water baths. This removes some of the sericin that binds them together (see p. 8).

Then skilled operators carefully unwind the cocoons, today generally using reeling machines. The machines use moving brushes to catch the end of the cocoons' silken strands. The thin, strong silk filaments are then pulled onto revolving wheels, which collect the unwound silk. The resulting silk, which still contains most of its binding sericin, is called *raw silk*.

As each cocoon comes close to the end of the unwinding process, the reeling machine operator attaches the unbroken silk strand of a new cocoon. This makes the thread longer, usually about 700 yards to 1,300 yards.

These unwound silk strands are too thin to be used alone as silk

In modern silkmaking factories large reeling machines unwind the silk filaments from cocoons. During the unwinding process skilled operators attach the beginning of a new cocoon's filament to the end of an old one, so continuous threads result.

Silk that has been reeled and thrown is looped into large coils called *skeins*, like these in a modern Chinese silk factory. In the background a worker is tending a throwing machine.

process several newly made silk threads are twisted together to make them stronger. This twisting is done as the machine winds reeled silk threads into long, loose coils of thread called *skeins*.

The number and kind of twists (called *turns*) vary. That is because different kinds of silk fabrics call for different numbers of twists and tighter or looser turns.

At the end of the reeling and throwing processes, the result is skeins of several kinds of high-quality silk yarns. These go on to be woven into silk cloth (see p. 27).

Spun Silk

Silk that is not in continuous filaments—and therefore cannot be processed by reeling and throwing—is spun into silk yarn. This kind of silk comes from several sources. Most of it is short-filament silk out of cocoons set aside during the sorting process (see p. 22).

thread. Instead, three to ten strands are usually combined as they unwind. How many strands are combined depends on the desired thickness of the final thread.

Throwing

After reeling comes *throwing* (from an old English word *thrawan*, which means "twisting"). In this

Spun silk also includes the rough and uneven ends of long silk filaments. These pieces have been clipped off before reeling and just before the cocoon's unwinding has been completed.

Some spun silk comes from *floss*. This is the name for silk fragments brushed from cocoons while they are being sorted and prepared for reeling. Spun silk also includes *silk scrap*, bits and pieces of silk formed during manufacturing.

Although spun silk is real silk, it is not as strong, durable, and attractive as silk made from long, unbroken filaments. Being of poorer quality, spun silk costs less. It is used in several kinds of silk fabrics, silk sewing thread, and many home furnishing products.

Another kind of scrap is composed of waste silk thrown off while silk is being prepared for spinning. This is called *noil silk* or *waste silk*. This is a rough, low-quality silk used in some heavy draperies and home furnishings.

At the silk factory workers first sort the cocoons, setting aside those that are broken or damaged in any way. Silk from those cocoons will be spun into thread. The unbroken cocoons will be unwound into continuous long filaments.

"Wild silk" or silk that is broken or damaged must be spun into thread before it can be used. This woman in traditional Indian dress is spinning silk thread by hand in the traditional way at a silk-making festival in 2002.

Spun Wild Silk

Wild silk cocoons yield lower-quality short-filament silk. They cannot be reeled and thrown, like high-quality long-filament silk, but instead must be spun into yarn.

Wild silk cocoons are broken by escaping moths before the cocoons are gathered, making filaments short (see p. 10). Rough and more uneven, wild silks also have less luster than the silk made by the *Bombyx mori* silkworm. This is largely because wild silkworms are not as carefully cultivated. They feed mainly on oak leaves, rather than on high-quality mulberry leaves.

Spinning Silk

People have been spinning silk and other fibers into yarn for thousands of years. In ancient times this was done at home by hand and with very simple devices and machines. Some spinning is still done by hand in many parts of the world. Today, however, most spinning is done by machines in large factories.

Working in modern Iran, this weaver is using a traditional loom to weave bright and beautiful silk fabric.

However it is done, the process of spinning fiber into yarn (thread) remains basically the same. The fibers must be cleaned and straightened in preparation for spinning, worked together into the kinds of yarns wanted, and then wound onto spools ready to be used in weaving cloth.

First the silk is very carefully cleaned with repeated hot washes and drying to remove the remaining sericin. After that, in a series of operations, the silk is combed out, straightened, and formed into thin sheets and then strands (called *slivers*) ready to be spun into yarn.

While the silk is being readied for spinning, other materials, such as cotton or wool, may be added. This creates a mixed or *blended* fabric.

Near the end of these preparations, twists are added to the strands of silk, in a process called *roving*. Finally, the silk is spun into yarn.

Weaving Silk

Like spinning, weaving is a skill that was developed thousands of years ago. For most of those thou-

This is the highly magnified surface of some woven silk fabric, tinted green during the photography. It shows how the silk threads criss-cross each other to form cloth.

sands of years, weaving was done at home on a simple machine called a *loom*.

Some of the world's weaving is still done on small looms at home. Today, however, most weaving is done in large textile factories on far larger, faster, and more powerful looms than in ancient times.

The loom is basically a frame that holds two sets of threads. One set of threads, called the *warp* threads, are held tightly end-to-end in the loom. The loom sets the second set of threads, called the *weft* (or *filling*) threads, across the warp threads and pushes the weft threads into place. The resulting cross-threaded cloth is as solid and strong as the yarns in it and the number of threads that meet and lock together to make the cloth.

Although looms are different today, the kinds of weaves and the cloth they create are basically the same as those made by skilled weavers using primitive looms in ancient times. Today as yesterday, weavers create cloth of many colors, patterns, textures, and qualities.

Whether woven from high-quality skeins of long-filament silk or from spun silk yarn, silk cloth is made in a wide range of weaves. The two most common are the *plain weave*, the world's simplest and most widespread weave, and the *satin weave*, used for many of the world's most beautiful and costly clothing and artworks.

In the plain weave, the warp and weft (filling) yarns are interlaced at right angles on the loom. The result is a simple kind of cloth that is used in a very wide range of clothing and household goods. Silk shirts, many kinds of dresses, and curtains are a few of the hundreds of plain-weave silks made around the world.

Far from plain is the satin weave, which results in a smooth, lustrous outer surface and a dull inner one. This weave is used in highly prized, very expensive satin evening gowns, draperies, rugs, and velvets. Many expensive silks are done in very complicated *jacquard* weaves, named after the special jacquard loom.

Silk is also used in many other weaves and in some kinds of knit clothing. There are silk ties, suits, slippers, scarves, sweaters, bedspreads, and much else. Silk is also blended with many other fabrics, including cotton, wool, linen, and many synthetic fabrics.

Most silk fabric today is woven on huge machines like this one in Bangladesh. The finished material may be used for clothing, draperies, furniture coverings, and much more.

Words to Know

Bombyx mori The variety of SILKWORM moth that creates the high-quality silks originally made famous by China.

cocoon A temporary shelter spun of silk threads, protecting the SILKWORM as it changes into a moth. In SERICULTURE the silkworm is killed before the moth emerges, to keep the threads unbroken.

fibroin The main PROTEIN in silk.

filament The long, continuous silken thread formed by the SILKWORM. Broken threads are called *short filaments*.

filature A silk factory, where silk from cocoons is unwound and converted into thread.

filling: See WEFT.

floss Silk fragments brushed from COCOONS when they are being prepared for REELING.

larva (plural: larvae) The caterpillar stage in the life cycle of the SILKWORM moth.

loom The basic tool used in WEAVING, which holds the WARP and WEFT yarns in place as they are cross-threaded to form cloth.

luster The quality of reflecting light. Fine silks are naturally lustrous.

muga silk: See WILD SILK.

noil silk (waste silk) A low-quality silk thrown off as silk is prepared for SPINNING.

plain weave The most used basic weave, in which the WARP and WEFT yarns are interlaced at right angles to each other.

proteins Substances found in all living cells, made of carbon, hydrogen, oxygen, nitrogen, and often sulfur. Silk is mainly made of the proteins FIBROIN and SERICIN.

raw silk Silk FILAMENTS that have been unwound during the REELING process but still contain most of their SERICIN.

reeling The process of unwinding the silk FILA-MENTS of the SILKWORM COCOONS, ideally without breaking them, once done wholly by hand, now more often done by machine.

roving The process of adding additional twists to silk yarn being prepared for SPINNING.

satin weave A weave (see WEAVING) that results in a smooth, lustrous outer surface and a dull inner one.

serica: See SERICULTURE.

sericin A PROTEIN that coats the silk thread formed mainly of FIBROIN. The gumlike sericin holds the threads together in the COCOON and is removed during processing.

sericulture The process of cultivating (tending and feeding) SILKWORMS so that they produce silks of the desired quality. *Serica* was an early Greek word for silk.

short filaments: See FILAMENT.

Silk Road A historic trading route that stretched across Asia between China and the Mediter-ranean. Silk was its main product for centuries.

silkworm The caterpillar (*larva*) form of silkworm moths, primarily the BOMBYX MORI variety. It pro-duces the silk threads through SPINNERETS.

skeins: See THROWING.

slivers Strands of silk as prepared for SPINNING.

spinnerets Two glands below the mouth of the SILK-WORM. They produce the liquid that hardens to become silk FILAMENTS.

spinning The process of twisting short FILAMENTS of silk into a thread of roughly even width, result-ing in *spun silk*. Long-filament silk does not need to be spun because it is naturally a thread.

spun silk: See SPINNING.

throwing Following REELING, the process of twisting several silk threads together to make them stronger. The number and kind of twists (called *turns*) depends on the type of woven fabric desired. The resulting thread is formed into long, loose coils called *skeins*.

turns: See THROWING.

tussah silk: See WILD SILK.

warp The lengthwise yarns held in place by a LOOM during WEAVING.

weaving The process of making cloth out of threads on a LOOM.

weft (filling) The crosswise yarns held in place by a LOOM during WEAVING, to be interlaced with the WARP yarns.

weighting Adding chemicals to silk to make it heavier.

wild silk Silks from SILKWORMS other than the BOM-BYX MORI variety. These silkworms are not actually wild but have been cultivated. The most common wild silks are *tussah silk* and *muga silk*.

On the Internet

The Internet has many interesting sites about silk. The site addresses often change, so the best way to find current addresses is to go to a search site, such as www.yahoo.com. Type in a word or phrase, such as "silk."

As this book was being written, websites about silk included:

http://www.fabrics.net/silk.asp
A section of Fabrics.Net focusing on silk, with information about different kinds of silk and fabrics woven from it.

http://www.interlog.com/~gwhite/ttt/tttintro.html
Textiles Through Time, a private website of links relating to textiles.

http://char.txa.cornell.edu/
Art, Design, and Visual Thinking, a site from Cornell University offering information about fibers, yarns, and design using them.

In Print

Your local library system will have various books on silk. The following is just a sampling of them.

Anquetil, Jean. *Silk*. Paris: Flammarion, 1995.

Burnham, Dorothy K. *Warp and Weft*. Toronto: Royal Ontario Museum, 1980.

Corbman, Bernard P. *Textiles: Fiber to Fabric*. New York: McGraw-Hill, 1983.

Feltwell, John. *The Story of Silk*. New York: St. Martin's, 1990.

Franck, Irene M., and David M. Brownstone. *The Silk Road: A History*. New York: Facts On File, 1986.

Hecht, Ann. *The Art of the Loom*. New York: Rizzoli, 1989.

Kadolph, Sara J., and Anna L. Langford. *Textiles*. Upper Saddle River, NJ: Prentice-Hall, 1998.

Lasky, Kathryn. *The Weaver's Gift*. New York: Frederick Warne, 1980.

Scott, Philippa. *The Book of Silk*. London: Thames and Hudson, 1993.

Textiles: 5,000 Years. Jennifer Harris, ed. New York: Harry N. Abrams, 1993.

Van Nostrand's Scientific Encyclopedia, 8th ed., 2 vols. Douglas M. Considine and Glenn D. Considine, eds. New York: Van Nostrand Reinhold, 1995.

Wilton, Kax. *A History of Textiles*. Boulder, CO: Westview Press, 1979.

Wingate, Isabel B. *Textile Fibers and Their Selection*. Englewood Cliffs, NJ: Prentice-Hall, 1976.

Index